10 Mistakes to Avoid When Buying Your Next Car

THIS BOOK COULD SAVE YOU THOUSANDS OF DOLLARS ON YOUR NEXT AUTO PURCHASE

TYWONE THOMAS

10 Mistakes to Avoid When Buying Your Next Car
ISBN1451585349 EAN-139781451585346

Published by T.Thomas Communications
Lawrenceville, GA USA
info@tthomascommunications.com

Printed in the United States of America

Edited by Shirley Voorhees
Cover design and print production by Riverstone Group, LLC

T.Thomas Communications and this author are in no way responsible for any loss incurred by an individual using this information or any of the services suggested herein.

Disclaimer: We are in no way affiliated with the websites suggested. They are simply our recommendations.

Acknowledgements

God - Thank you for blessing me. My desire is for your light to shine in all that I do.

My wife Vanessa - You are my gift from God and I love you so much. Thank you for being my beautiful wife and the mother of my children. Gold cannot compare to your worth and value to me.

Jordan and Eden -You two are very special to me. Thanks for allowing Daddy to write and work on this book. Don't ever put limits on your dreams!

Sandra Smith - I love you, Momma. Thanks for displaying the heart of a warrior and not showing fear, but stepping out to try new things. I have inherited the heart of a champion.

James & Elizabeth Burks - Words cannot describe what you mean to me. Thank you for raising the wonderful, smart, beautiful woman who agreed to be my wife. She has truly changed my life and I am forever grateful. You both are very thoughtful and I am so happy to be part of your family.

Jon & Debra Carr - Thank you for the years of advice and counsel. Thank you for believing in me since I was a teenager.

Bobby Malone - Thanks for the encouragement to write this book and for your example.

Our V-group - Each of you is very special to my family. Thanks for allowing us to have a place to grow and for all of the friendships.

Georgia Federal Credit Union - One of the best credit unions in the world. Thank you for allowing me to serve each of you and your members.

Car Solutions - Steve, thanks for giving me the opportunity to use my gift in helping people through your organization. Thanks to each of the staff at Car Solutions for your encouragement and friendship.

Dan Miller - Thank you for your great advice and for helping me with this book. Your podcasts are practical and inspirational.

Eric Canaday - Thank you for your contribution to this book.

Table of Contents

Foreword

Thank you for your interest in this book. It is my goal to equip you with information that will save you time and money when shopping for your next vehicle.

Having worked in this industry for many years, I have seen the common mistakes that people often make when purchasing a vehicle. My goal is to provide you with knowledge that will assist you in car buying and help you avoid the same mistakes.

Please understand that sales people and dealerships are not your enemy. It is the lack of knowledge and understanding of practical, car buying information that is the enemy. It is not my intent to cast car dealers or sales people in a bad light. Many of them are honest and genuine in their commitment to offer great service at a fair price. However, you still need to be armed with knowledge and practical tools while shopping for your next vehicle in order to ensure that you get the best deal possible.

I suggest that you take this book with you the next time you go car shopping. You may even want to ask your sales-person for a few moments and step away to review the suggestions in this book before signing on the dotted line. This will allow you time to be certain that you are getting everything you want. Taking that moment has the potential to save you hundreds, if not thousands, of dollars.

If you find this information valuable, please consider sending your family and friends a copy of this "how-to" book so that they don't make mistakes that may cost them dearly.

Thanks and enjoy!

Tywone Thomas

1 Mistake

Shopping without pre-approval

Whether looking to buy a new or used vehicle, it is important to get pre-approved for a loan before going to a dealership. The whole car buying process will be made easier for you and for the sales agent helping you. You will feel more assured throughout the process knowing the bottom line number and financial parameters that meet your budget. And, your sales agent will be able to focus on helping you find the vehicle that matches your specifications rather than having to spend time working to get you financed once you arrive at the dealership.

Getting pre-approved also eliminates the possibility of frustration and embarrassment should you find a car you really want but fail to qualify for financing.

A gentleman once came to me from out of town to buy a car. He had spoken to someone at a credit union about a loan before traveling to meet with me. However, he did not have everything confirmed for his credit union membership, nor was he pre-approved before he arrived at the dealership. The vehicle he was interested in had been chosen and serviced before he ever left his home. What should have only taken about 30 minutes to complete, instead took an entire day as we waited for confirmation of loan approval.

You will save yourself wasted time and frustration by checking with your credit union or bank to receive pre-approval before visiting a dealership. And, just as you would determine the cost of construction before building a home, it is wise to know what your payment and terms are before searching for your new or used vehicle.

It is also important to consider the terms and interest rates that the credit union is willing to offer you. For example: On models two years old or less, the credit union may be willing to give you the same interest rate that they would give for a brand new vehicle. For our illustration here, let's say that they offer a rate of 4.95% for a term of 60 months. However, on models older than two years, they may be willing to give you their used car rate of 6.95% for only a 48 month term. Now you must consider whether it would be in your best interest to buy a newer model vehicle or one that is older.

This decision made before-hand will save you time at the dealership. You can tell your sales agent which age models you want to look at in order to take advantage of your credit union's best rate.

If you do not take the time to check with your credit union before shopping, you may find a model that you love, but be unable to get the loan and terms that fit your monthly payment limit. Then you will have wasted time and may be forced to start the process all over again.

Note: The rates and terms listed are only for illustration. Please contact your credit union or lending institution for their current rates and terms.

Mistake 2

Purchasing a used vehicle without mechanic inspection

You have been shopping around at several reputable used car lots and have found the car you want. It looks great and the salesperson assures you that it has been checked out and serviced. You take his word for it and sign the papers. The deal is sealed and you excitedly drive away in your pre-owned vehicle.

After driving it for a few days, you begin to notice that something is wrong. There is a noise coming from the tires. The tread had looked fine on the outside of them when you bought the car. However, your heart sinks as you take a closer look and realize that some of the tires need to be replaced because the inside of the tires is badly worn.

This is a true story and one that was avoidable. By simply taking the time to have the car inspected by a licensed mechanic before purchasing it, this person could have saved herself the aggravation.

A vehicle may look fine at first glance. However, if it has been in an accident, there may be damage that only a trained eye can see. There could also be problems under the hood that you cannot detect. Therefore, I recommend that you take the time to have a reputable mechanic look over any used car you intend to purchase.

It is a good idea to take the vehicle to its manufacturing dealer (e.g. a Ford to a Ford dealership). The dealer's service department mechanic may be familiar with problems particular to that make and model that would not be known to someone else. It will cost you a little for them to give you a full written inspection, but it will be well worth it. This written inspection can afford you the opportunity to negotiate with the dealer in the event that any problems are found.

I recommend, too, that you ask to drive the car for a day so that you have a chance to notice anything else that may need to be fixed...things that may be overlooked otherwise. You may also want to request a copy of the service report of things the dealer did to the vehicle before they offered it for sale.

The person in my story returned to the dealership where she purchased her vehicle and they agreed to pay half the price of the new tires. Had she taken the time to have the car checked out beforehand, she could have negotiated a set of new tires at no cost to her at all. If the dealer had really wanted to close the deal, he would have been willing to replace the tires in order to get the sale.

Be smart in the purchase of your next vehicle and remember this important step. It could save you money and frustration in the long-run!

Note: I recommend that you not use a "back yard" mechanic or have a friend who is somewhat knowledgeable about cars give you an opinion as to the reliability of the vehicle you consider purchasing. Use a professional so that you get professional results. Anyone else may miss problems that would be obvious to a licensed mechanic.

Mistake 3

Accepting the first offer

Whether purchasing a new or pre-owned vehicle, shop and compare. I recommend getting two or three quotes on a particular vehicle before making your decision.

This is especially good advice when looking to buy a used vehicle. The dealer's purchase price can vary depending upon where they purchased it and how much they spent.

Let's imagine that you are shopping for a Honda CRV. At the first dealership you find one selling for $19,000. However, taking this advice to shop and compare, you visit another dealership and find the same car, offering the same options, at $17,000. Dealer A could have purchased their vehicle for $17,000, while Dealer B may have only paid $15,000 for theirs. Dealer A may also have had to make repairs that the second dealer did not, driving up the asking price.

If you do not shop and compare before buying, you could end up paying more for your vehicle than is necessary.

When shopping for a new vehicle, I recommend getting at least three quotes. Feel free to use the Auto Shopping Worksheet at the end of this book so that you can organize your quotes from different dealers. Also take note of how the sales person is treating you. If he/she does not return your calls, leaves you with a feeling of distrust, speaks to you unprofessionally, or has an attitude, you may want to think twice about doing business there, even if the deal they offer seems good.

Note: A vehicle may be $1000 less expensive than a competitor's car but may have some mechanical issues. Remember that you get what you pay for. Just because the vehicle is cheaper doesn't mean that it is the best deal for you. Do not always put price before quality and service!

Mistake 4

Not getting a vehicle history report

A gentleman who had once purchased a used car and was ready to sell it, called me for some advice. I encouraged him to take the vehicle to a dealership that I knew purchased used cars and that would typically write a check for it right on the spot. Upon inspection, however, the gentleman was told that the vehicle had been in a previous accident and that would reduce the value of the car. This was a surprise to him! He had no knowledge of that previous accident because he had not requested a vehicle history report before purchasing it. The car had been clean and looked to be in good condition.

It can be a very disheartening experience to be offered less for your car than you expected. Therefore, always request a vehicle history report. Most dealers will provide you with a free report upon request. If they do not have one, you may purchase a report from either carfax.com or autocheck.com. The report will let you know if the vehicle has ever been in an accident that has been reported to the Department of Motor Vehicle; how many previous owners it may have had; if an airbag has ever deployed; if the car has been flooded; had odometer problems; is a lemon; was a rental vehicle; and its origin. Also, check the date of the report to make sure that it is recent. If it is not, something could have happened to the vehicle between the date of the report and the time you receive it.

Be aware that the report you receive may not offer a full history. However, some information is better than none at all!

Note: Just because a vehicle has an accident report, does not necessarily mean it is a bad car or a lemon. If you really like the vehicle, have it inspected to make sure there are no major issues. However, if a report shows that an airbag has been deployed, that is a red flag and I would recommend thinking twice before buying it.

5 Mistake

Paying over dealer's invoice price

(Refers to new cars only)

Before you go shopping for a new car, do your homework. Decide on a make and model you think you would enjoy and then go online to carsdirect.com, cars.com, and other like websites, to find what the invoice and rebates are on those particular vehicles. Then when you visit a dealership, you will be prepared. As you begin negotiations, remember that the MSRP*, or sticker price, is not the place to start. Begin instead at the dealer's invoice number. In fact, I recommend that you ask the dealer for a printed copy of the invoice with the VIN** number listed on it. NEVER pay over invoice, if at all possible. And, never pay the MSRP for a vehicle, no matter how much you love it! Your goal should be to pay the invoice price minus any rebates that are available.

Note: If a dealer is not willing to sell you a new vehicle for invoice minus rebates, walk away from the deal. There are plenty of other dealers who may be hungrier for your business.

*MSRP- Manufactured Suggested Retail Price

**VIN- Vehicle Identification Number

Mistake 6

Showing too much emotion at the dealership

Attention, first time buyers!!

As a first time buyer, it would be easy for you to be taken advantage of by a salesperson, unless you are educated about the process. That is why I have written this book – to educate you.

When you find the vehicle you have been looking for, it is difficult not to show your enthusiasm over it, especially if it is your first car. However, if you gush about how excited you are and how much you love the car, you may diminish your negotiating power with your salesperson.

First time buyers also have a tendency to focus only on the payment figure they have in mind. Do not tell a salesperson to do whatever they can to get you into the car you want as long as your payment is a certain figure (e.g. $300 per month). Make sure that you look at all of the numbers and not the payment only. It is not uncommon for extra fees and accessories to be added to the vehicle in order for the dealer to make more profit and yet still keep your payment at the desired figure by extending the terms of the deal.

Here is a list of the only charges that should be on a buyer's order:

Selling Price

Dealer Documentation Fee (if required or allowed in your state)

Taxes

Tag & Title Fee

Lemon Law Fee (only if it is a new car and applicable in your state)

Extended Warranty (only if you choose)

*GAP Insurance (if you choose)

Remember, if you "show your hand" too soon, your salesperson may be less willing to negotiate to your desired level. Reserve your excitement and enthusiasm for afterwards when you have been able to get your best deal and are driving away in your brand new car!

*GAP - Guaranteed Auto Protection

7 Mistake

Accepting dealer's GAP Insurance and Extended Warranties

The car buying process can be a long and tedious one. By the time you sit down to negotiate and "do the math," it is common to be exhausted and ready to be finished with the whole experience. It is at this point that you need to be the most alert and careful.

Frequently, car-buyers have a payment figure in mind and as long as the final figure fits within those parameters, they will agree to whatever suggestions the salesperson makes concerning GAP insurance and extended warranties. Yet, this is a mistake. As I have said before, do your homework! Shop around to make sure that you are getting the best price.

Another common mistake is to go to the company who already provides your car insurance because the fees can be figured into your existing monthly payment. I recommend checking with your local credit union before agreeing to any such arrangement with the dealer or your insurance company.

I once knew a couple who made this very mistake. They had visited a dealership and fell in love with a pre-owned vehicle. They were so focused on the bottom-line that they failed to get a break down of all the add-ons that the dealer was charging them. Because everything fit within their budget, they agreed to the GAP insurance and extended warranty through the dealer and the deal was done.

When I spoke with the gentleman the next day, I realized that they had made two mistakes: 1) they had paid too much for the vehicle to begin with, and 2) they had paid too much for the GAP insurance and warranty product that had been sold to them. I connected them with a credit union that was able to save them about $1,000 for both products combined.

This is another reason I recommend using a credit union, so that you can keep the car buying experience separate from car financing.

Being a savvy car buyer will help you save money and get the best deal possible.

8 Mistake

Not looking at all of your options

If you are looking for a used vehicle, you may want to consider purchasing from a private owner, through one of the available online websites or the classified ads in your local newspaper. There are some great deals offered by private sellers that could possibly save you money. And, one of the benefits of such a purchase is that you may not have to pay sales tax, depending on where you live. Different states have different tax laws.

Some of the most popular websites you may want to check out are autotrader.com, craigslist.com and ebay.com. (See page 45 for a complete list.)

I especially recommend buying from a private seller if your

purchase price is $5,000 or less. Many used car dealerships' prices will be significantly higher than that.

Should you decide to take this suggestion, please remember to have the vehicle inspected by a licensed mechanic before buying it. It is not uncommon for someone to sell their car because of mechanical issues and you certainly do not want to inherit those troubles!

9 Mistake

Buying at the beginning of the month

Buying at the beginning of the month may not be the wisest choice. Dealerships and their sales staff have quotas each month and they may work harder to sell you a car toward the end of the month if their quota has not yet been met. This is often when you can get a better deal.

Watch the television and newspaper for ads about sales that may be occurring in your area. Any time of the month can be a good time to buy, if the deal is right. Just be aware that buying at the end of the month may be your best option.

And, as a sidebar note, do not necessarily believe that waiting until the end of the year is the best time to buy because of

"Year End" deals. Many times that is a promotional gimmick. A "Year End" may be in March when a dealership is preparing to roll out the next year's model. That may be when the manufacturer offers special rebates or incentives on the current year in order to move their inventory. Remember: "Year End" can be celebrated throughout the year!

10 Mistake

Failing to get everything you want

It is very important to make sure that everything you want is included in your negotiations for a vehicle before completing the sale. For instance, one woman wanted an extra key and floor mats for the vehicle she was purchasing. Before she "sealed the deal," she got an agreement from the salesperson that they would be included. Had she waited until the sale was complete, do you suppose she would have gotten them? Probably not. If you want something, ask for it before signing all the papers. You may not always get what you have asked for, but you will be more likely to get it if you ask beforehand than you will if you wait until the deal is done. The salesperson will feel no obligation to help you then.

Q&A

Answers to some of the most common questions related to car buying.

1. What is the first thing that I should consider before visiting a dealership?

There are many makes and models of vehicles available. Before you visit a dealer, do a little research and decide what type of vehicle will best suit your needs and desires. Are there specific features you just must have? When you have narrowed it down, plant that decision firmly in your mind because once you arrive at the dealership, the dealer will often try to sell you what they have in inventory even though it may not meet your needs or specifications. If you have not taken this step, you will likely be subject to emotional buying and not make a choice that you will be satisfied with later.

If you have made a decision as to the make and model that best meets your needs and one dealer does not have what you are looking for, don't panic! There are other dealerships out there. Keep searching until you find exactly what you need and want.

2. How will I know that I am getting a good deal?

When you have done your homework and research, you will be able to tell that you are getting a good deal. Remember that your salesperson may be the nicest and most honest person in the world, but your trust should be in your research. Salespeople have quotas and goals to reach, so they may try to steer you toward a purchase that is more in their best interest than yours.

People often get taken advantage of because they have not taken the time, or perhaps don't know where to go, in order to get the information they need to make a great deal.

The internet is a wonderful resource for information about vehicles and prices. Before you start shopping, research is a must if you want to be certain that the deal you are offered is a good one.

3. Is it better to lease or buy a vehicle?

I recommend buying and not leasing for personal use. Many people focus on payments only. And, some prefer to drive a more expensive car than they could afford to buy in order to impress their family and friends so they decide to lease (rent) a car instead.

If you are debating this option, please remember that at the end of a lease you either turn in the car, use it as a trade with negative equity (in most cases), or turn the lease into a purchase. If you lease the vehicle, and turn it in, you have nothing to show for the money you have paid. If you buy a car instead, you then have the option later to either sell it or use it in a trade for your next vehicle.

4. Should I trade in my vehicle to a dealership or sell it on my own to an individual?

There are pros and cons to this issue. If you sell your vehicle to an individual, you stand to make more money on it than you would from trading it. I would recommend posting your vehicle on popular websites like autotrader.com or your local newspaper websites. However, you must determine if you want to deal with the haggle and hassles that can come from selling your vehicle on your own.

If you don't have the time to handle this course of action, or are not savvy about the process, it may be better to trade in your vehicle at the dealership. I recommend getting two or three appraisals from different dealers to see who will give you the most money for the trade.

Should you decide to trade in your vehicle, you can take advantage of a tax savings. For example, the taxable amount on a new vehicle may be $25,000. If your trade-in amount is $10,000, then your new taxable amount would be $15,000, offering you a considerable tax advantage.

5. Should I finance with the dealer, use online financing, or go to my local credit union?

My suggestion is that you check with your local credit union first because they may have some of the best rates available. I prefer working with credit unions because of their relational approach to banking. They look at their members' situations and not just the numbers only.

Time after time I have seen people get taken advantage of by a dealership and then have to go back to their credit union, asking them to help clean up the mistakes they made.

Be sure to check with your credit union first.

6. New or used...which should I buy?

What you want to accomplish determines whether you buy a new or used vehicle. Do you just need a vehicle to get you from one place to another, or do you want to have something with good trade-in value later down the road?

If you are buying pre-owned, always check to see what the prices are on a new model before making your final decision because some vehicles hold their value more than others. It may be better for you to buy a new vehicle with its current rebates, incentives, and warranties. But, again, make sure to do your research before making a purchase!

7. How do I check to see if a vehicle is still under the manufacturer's warranty?

You can find out by calling the service department at your local dealer. Give them the VIN (Vehicle Identification Number) for the make of car that you are considering. They should be able to tell you if it is still under warranty.

Please keep in mind that some manufacturers offer a 100,000 mile warranty, but that in most cases those are not bumper-to-bumper warranties. Most of those warranties are for the drive train only. (The drive train is mainly the engine and transmission of a vehicle.) Vehicles usually come with a smaller bumper-to-bumper warranty that is good up to 36,000 miles or 50,000 miles.

Keep in mind, too, that if you are buying a used car, the 100,000 mile warranty that may be offered on a new car may not apply to the used vehicle that you are considering. Some manufacturers state that if you are a second owner of the vehicle, you lose the 100,000 mile warranty and it drops down to 60,000 miles instead. Just be sure to ask specific questions to make certain that the perspective vehicle you are considering is still under warranty and you have a clear understanding of exactly what that means.

8. Are extended warranties any good?

Yes, however it depends on which one you choose. Be very careful to check the history of the warranty company to ensure that it is reputable. I would recommend doing an online search to find out if there are negative comments from previous buyers posted online.

Getting a warranty for your vehicle is like getting car insurance. It is good to have just in case something ever happens. I recommend getting one that has no deductible requirement. Shop around so that you get the best price.

If you have money in the bank to fix problems that may arise with your car, you may consider not purchasing an extended warranty. You have to decide what is best for you.

9. Should I get GAP insurance?

If you are not putting a substantial amount of money down on your purchase, you should buy GAP insurance. In the event of an accident, it will pay off a vehicle that is totaled by your insurance company in which they give you less money than your payoff price would be. The GAP Insurance will pay the difference between your payoff and what the insurance company is giving you.

However, I strongly encourage you not to buy GAP insurance from the dealer without checking with your local credit union first. This effort could save you money.

There is no need to get GAP insurance if you are paying cash for a vehicle or paying a large down payment.

10. Is it okay to buy from a local broker?

Yes, but remember to check references and be very careful. Some brokers may try to sell you a vehicle sight unseen. Never commit to a vehicle or put a down payment on one until you have seen the vehicle and had it checked out by a licensed mechanic.

Also, if a broker does not charge you taxes, do not complete the deal! The law requires that taxes be paid and if the broker is not following the laws set in place by the government, then chances are they may not be trustworthy and you should not trust them.

11. Where do I go to find values of new and used vehicles?

You can visit www.nada.com and www.kbb.com for new and used vehicle values. Please keep in mind that just because the book value states that you should get a certain amount for your trade, that does not mean that is what you will be offered. It may be less at a dealership because they look at the wholesale market values. Dealers usually pay close to the loan value of a vehicle which is very close to wholesale.

12. Does the vehicle you are interested in take regular or premium gas?

It is very important, especially if you are concerned about gas mileage, to check and see what grade of gasoline your prospective vehicle takes before agreeing to purchase. Make sure to do your research ahead of time. You do not want to be surprised when you have made a purchase and pull into the gas station for the first time.

13. When buying a new or used vehicle, if I have a trade in, should I keep my old tag or get a new one?

I would encourage you to take your tag even if you don't transfer your tag to your new vehicle. If you leave your tag on your trade in, you run the risk of someone possibly taking your tag and being reckless with it, leaving you responsible for their actions. Make sure to get your tag!

Helpful Websites

Carfax.com

Autocheck.com

Nada.com

Kbb.com

Edmunds.com

Carsdirect.com

Autotrader.com

Craigslist.com

Cars.com

Vehix.com

Consumerreports.org

Ripoffreport.com

Jdpower.com

Auto Shopping Worksheet

	MSRP	Invoice	Drive out Price *(including tax, tag & all dealer fees)*
Dealer 1			
Dealer 2			
Dealer 3			

Notes:

5124341R0

Made in the USA
Charleston, SC
03 May 2010